BICYCLE THIEVES

MARY DI MICHELE

a misFit book

Published by ECW Press
665 Gerrard Street East
Toronto, Ontario, Canada M4M 1Y2
416-694-3348 / info@ecwpress.com

Get the eBook free!*
*proof of purchase required

Purchase the print edition
and receive the eBook free!
For details, go to ecwpress.com/eBook.

LIBRARY AND ARCHIVES CANADA
CATALOGUING IN PUBLICATION

Di Michele, Mary, 1949–, author
Bicycle thieves : poems / Mary di Michele.

ISSUED IN PRINT AND ELECTRONIC FORMATS.
ISBN 978-1-77041-370-2 (paperback)
ALSO ISSUED AS: 978-1-77305-012-6 (PDF)
978-1-77305-011-9 (ePUB)

Editor for the press: Michael Holmes/
a misFit book

MISFIT

Cover design: Rachel Ironstone
Cover photo: Courtesy of the author

I. TITLE.

PS8557.I55B53 2017   C811'.54
C2016-906362-3   C2016-906363-1

The publication of *Bicycle Thieves* has been generously supported by the Canada Council for the Arts which
last year invested $153 million to bring the arts to Canadians throughout the country, and by the Government
of Canada through the Canada Book Fund. *Nous remercions le Conseil des arts du Canada de son soutien. L'an
dernier, le Conseil a investi 153 millions de dollars pour mettre de l'art dans la vie des Canadiennes et des Canadiens
de tout le pays. Ce livre est financé en partie par le gouvernement du Canada.* We also acknowledge the Ontario Arts
Council (OAC), an agency of the Government of Ontario, which last year funded 1,709 individual artists and
1,078 organizations in 204 communities across Ontario, for a total of $52.1 million, and the contribution of the
Government of Ontario through the Ontario Book Publishing Tax Credit and the Ontario Media Development
Corporation.

ONTARIO ARTS COUNCIL
CONSEIL DES ARTS DE L'ONTARIO
an Ontario government agency
un organisme du gouvernement de l'Ontario

Canada Council
for the Arts

Conseil des Arts
du Canada

Canada

PRINTED AND BOUND IN CANADA   PRINTING: COACH HOUSE PRINTING   5   4   3   2   1

BICYCLE THIEVES

FOR MY MOTHER AND MY FATHER
AND FOR ALL THOSE WHO SEEK
TO SHAPE THEIR LIFE SENTENCES

The past beats inside me like a second heart.
— JOHN BANVILLE

SCOTOPIA   1

i **THE MONTREAL BOOK OF THE DEAD**   3
NOW HE DRIVES A TAXI IN COMOX   4
THE MOUNTAIN AFTER KLEIN   5
THE BICYCLE THIEF   7
IN ANOTHER LANGUAGE   9
THE WINDS OF HOMECOMING   10
LEFT BEHIND   14
FORGETFULNESS   15
THE UNTEACHABLE   17
THE MONTREAL BOOK OF THE DEAD   19
THE POSSIBILITY OF TIME TRAVEL   21
LA VITA VECCHIA   22
THE TASTE OF LOSS   24
. . . AND THEN SHE WOKE UP   25
TURNING THIRTY TWICE OVER   26
BLACK DOG   27

ii **LIFE SENTENCES**   29
LIFE SENTENCES
      (An Autobiography in Verse)   30

iii **AFTER**   51
LIKE KAFKA'S APE (After Giorgio Caproni)   52
THE LIGHT IN EACH OF US
      (After Giorgio Caproni)   53
EVENING LIGHT (After Umberto Saba)   54
THE BLUE BOWING OF EVENING
      (After Dino Campana)   55
ARS POETICA (After Dino Campana)   56
ON STYLE (After Dino Campana)   57
BED OF ROSES (After Dino Campana)   59
LIFE IS A ROSE (Ronsard V)   60
ON THE WAY TO THE VILLAGE STEAM BATHS
      (After Pier Paolo Pasolini)   61
THE BIG BANG   63
ENIGMATICO REVISITED   64
DE SICA'S *LADRI DI BICICLETTE*   65
ROBERT LOWELL READS AT SCARBOROUGH
      COLLEGE, CIRCA 1970   66
A POEM ABOUT ABSOLUTELY NOTHING   68
DEATH AND TRANSFIGURATION IN NEW YORK CITY
      (An Essay in Verse)   69
SOMEWHERE I HAVE NEVER TRAVELLED   79

Author's Notes   81
Acknowledgements   85

SCOTOPIA

Beacon shining from the top of Mount Royal,
a cross, unblinking under Capricorn.

Beaver Lake is iced over. The ring
in his pocket stays in his pocket.

In the shadow of the red-tailed hawk, what's left
of a crow is now just tail feathers and wings

splayed out in the arms of a maple. To look is
to look away. Where the earth is flat we forget

we walk on a planet, but, from the view
at the summit, we remember

we are not alone, married and unmarried
alike, the stellar bridegroom

orbiting above, astronaut or angel,
watches over us from the stratosphere.

In a flash — we see what he sees — the city
below from space: the mystery

illuminated. This island city — this
island, Earth. Animal or mineral,

we all bow to the darkness,
we all turn in the light.

THE MONTREAL
BOOK OF THE DEAD

Still to be so poised, so
Receptive. Still to recall, to praise.
— JAMES MERRILL

NOW HE DRIVES A TAXI IN COMOX

He remembers the darkness of winter
mornings when he was fifteen and helped
the milkman deliver milk door-to-door.
The wagon was drawn by a horse, hooves

on cobblestone, the only sound, and the milkman
humming under his breath while the boy
he was would run up to each house, a bottle
of milk in his hand, the glass slick with cold,

the wagon waiting, the horse stomping.
That was 1954, and before
the milkman bought his first truck; before
his father's last transfer to the airbase

here in Comox. Now as he drives the taxi,
I transport him back — though nearly sixty years
have passed since those icy mornings, the boy
in him wakes up. Montreal is beckoning,

the city, luminous in his mind; he can see again
the copper dome of St. Joseph's Cathedral
rising newly polished against the sky and not
blanched by snow and passing time.

THE MOUNTAIN AFTER KLEIN

I who first knew it as a dark stage for the shining
white cross in celluloid, with the reel
moon by its side, hovering
in the cobalt air of Arcand's *Jésus of Montréal*,
did not know the mountain at all, regarding
what was only the patina of the movie poster.

When I moved to Montreal at forty
I was young. It was easy then climbing
up its gentle slopes, clambering
all the way to the top to see the beacon
cross up close, where it was
unmasked, a charade of tin and wire
surrounded by a chain-link fence,
though at night, switched on, it lit the way,
declared to all: "I am not Toronto,
I am the full and unwaning moon for this metro-
polis of snow."

In its layers the mountain keeps, not hours,
but geological time. In Mont Royal
find not a mount at all really
but a hill
of the Monteregian hills.

This fall the maples are ubiquitous, and in their regalia
of red and gold, blazing the mountain's flanks.
O the amber light of abbreviated afternoons!
Montreal, my autumn will always be spent

with you. This November day, lazing
in amazing sunshine, thinking about "The Mountain,"
the Cartier Monument, where Klein and Lefty play hooky
and throw gravel against the bronze tits of Justice,
as I sit in Place Norman Bethune, by the sandblasted
figure of a man who spat on injustice.
He stands alone and unadorned, still striving forward
for the good of mankind. Such gravitas —
except that someone has put dark glasses on him.

Come spring I will climb the mountain
at night and, as if stepping into a film screen,
pale as Robert Lepage,
join the spring pageantry of pain,
carrying my coat as I warm up,
and visit the cross, illuminated, and illuminating
the city megaliths, the towers, the bridges, the river,
and even through the darkness and distance I will see
the old port, where cruise ships dock, and Jésus is
a sailor, walking on the water,
while revellers, all dressed in white, toast —
hooray and apocalypse —
His coming, their going.

THE BICYCLE THIEF

If I could go back to my birthplace, Lanciano,
wander all day up and down the *corso*,
stop by the cathedral built on the ruins
of a Roman prison and pray,
                                        if I could

make my way at night by the glimmering
of my brief candle, and if I could see
into the darkness and find my father,
if he were still living
                                        there in Lanciano.

Strangely it seems it was just yesterday
that I returned from Lanciano feeling
despondent because if I were pure
spirit I could have gone back
                                        in time too

(traversed the years along with the miles),
and so have seen my father before
the World War, seen the boy my father was
before his father betrayed
                                        a barefoot son

and sold his bicycle. If I call him
by his true name, Vincenzo, not Vincent,
will he recall then his life in Italian,
through eyes still clear,
                                        through hopes undimmed?

If I were sharper, or indeed purer,
I might yet see that boy in the old man
in stocking feet at the nursing home
in Toronto, my father who

                                 no longer knows

his life or his daughter in any language.
When at last he rises from his wheelchair,
when he leaves this earth to return to
earth, he too will go back

                            to Lanciano,

to the cathedral on the *corso*,
where he will find his bicycle among
the stolen years of his life, and ride it,
not towards the future, but into

                                 the past.

IN ANOTHER LANGUAGE

"I don't need anything. I'm fine here. Take care
of yourself." The last words your mother speaks
the last time you see her. Why was her death
the next day such a surprise? Did you not hear
the note of farewell in her voice? You remember

her words but translated. *Sto bene qui*, you wanted
to believe that. *Badete*. The wellness of where

she has gone.

THE WINDS OF HOMECOMING

The inner — what is it?
if not intensified sky
— RILKE (STEPHEN MITCHELL TRANSLATION)

i A Visitor to My Home

Cast away like fingernail clippings,
sloughed off with pumice like calluses,
swept up with tendrils of hair from salon floors,
these small losses are no loss at all, no,
they cannot prepare us to see her snatched
from herself, the body itself discarded
and set aside in a box. We did not
   see you leave it behind, Mamma.

I remember my sister's long hair, her thick
braided pigtails cut off for the first time.
Mother saved one in a shoebox where it
lay hidden in a dresser drawer and forgotten.
Many years later, a visitor to my home,
I found it. The braid itself had no memory
of my sister though, glinting, quick with copper
   lights, it seemed the memory itself

of childhood, something almost alive, something
once combed and braided by Mother, bent
patiently over her youngest child, her hands, tender,
capable, combing out the snags, plaiting
the hair that would fly up while playing
   those skipping games.

ii The Viewing

Hands, folded at the waist, fingers, entwined
with a black rosary, stiff in unprayer,
the beads glistening with tears not her own,
those hands that were my mother's are so cold,
       cold to the core.

They have stopped their incessant folding of
napkin, paper, fabric, her skirt now all
smooth. She is dressed in brown brocade, stylish,
she who was modest with few clothes and wore
no jewellery, a use has been found for her cameo
pin, its silhouette of a woman's face,
       pinched and made strange.

I kiss the icy cheek. Something in me
cleaves, that something in me denies, insists
that's not my mother. I whisper goodbye
       to the gone.

iii　The Burial

She is no longer with us. These are called, rightly,
earthly remains, what is left of her, what
is put in the ground at Prospect Cemetery.

The cross, the metal Christ, must not be buried
with her. Disrespectful to suggest it,
sacrilegious to wish it. But He who
brought back his friend Lazarus from the tomb
　　　　　never saw His mother dead.

The priest dispensed what looked like sand. We dropped
roses in January on the casket.
　　　　　　　　　　　And then we left.

in Postscript

Another winter and I find white cotton gloves,
the pallbearer pair, in the pockets of my good
wool coat. They are tarnished, soiled not with earth
               but with varnish.

Outside, the brightness of morning, blue sky, another
New Year's Day she will not greet. I refuse
to turn up my collar against the cold, to button

the buttons, imagining something of my mother might be
            felt there — welcoming the *winds of homecoming*.

LEFT BEHIND

She wakes up again beside her sleeping child,
                    the book of fairy tales lies
open on the floor. In the kitchen she pours,

                              over ice, a mere thimbleful
of scotch. Why be so abstemious?
                    But still she is. Silence is the sound

of clinking from her glass. Stepping out onto the deck,
                    really just a fire escape, iron and rusting,
sipping the drink, she inhales deeply the night air,

                    taking in the smells, metallic, putrid,
wafting up from the landlady's yard.
She cannot see the chrysanthemums, the compost,

                    the trail left by the skunk rooting
for scraps. The moon is a bow the pale
huntress left behind. There are grown-up myths

as near, as distant now
                    as childhood's *forever after*,
                              dreaming in another room.

FORGETFULNESS

The house with the first number missing
from its door, and the fence falling down
to one side, backs onto the sea and glacier
topped mountains. The iodine air, the salt wind

blows in through windowpanes cracked and smeared
with birdlime. There are books in every room
of this house. In the kitchen you'll find Sappho,
in the bedroom, Basho,

by the vanity and the lone mirror
reflecting a steel framed single bed.
A woman lived alone here for many years,
one fond of scotch and poetry,

her only gentlemen callers that thrush
knocking insistently at the window
and an old man claiming to be her husband.
She would have none of him.

There's a spill on the rug she's come back
to clean up. But it's hard to see
in the dark and in any case the dead cannot clean.
The book she dropped,

though she bends to pick it up,
stays dropped. Useless
to return now as if in a forgetfulness
so profound, being dead could be forgotten too.

The old are like that. They told her: "memory
loss is part of the natural decline," they told her
not to worry. But the living,
the young, must work at forgetting, they must

deny, they must shut their eyes until the years
surprise them, bowed and trembling as they go
to pick up that book in the house
with one number missing from the door.

THE UNTEACHABLE

To be as if never born. Javier Marías
shows *The Dark Back of Time* to critics, cats
and dogs, pronouncing how little of what
they are will last. Perhaps because I teach

what, I am told, is unteachable,
I want to defend scholars, remind the writer
that even this stone I kick is more assuredly immortal
than Shakespeare. We are all palimpsests

for genomes: writers, critics, and our pets.
Rumi was long-lived for a cat, seventeen years.
And many years have passed along with him,
yet still, raising my eyes from a book of poetry,

not scratched up by his jealous claws,
I might see him, in the periphery
of my vision, the striped grey fur turning
a corner. Disappearing.

Buddy was the first to teach me to love
dogs, to trust them with my hand, my heart,
if not my muffins. What did I know?
I wanted a literary dog name, Bolden

from *Coming Through Slaughter*. Instead I was
given another way of being in the world,
away from the reading lamp, those long
evenings with him, ambling under stars,

walks in any weather. To be as if never
born. This cold Montreal spring, the run-off
iced over again, I am careful as I walk myself
across the park, not stopping to smell anything.

THE MONTREAL BOOK OF THE DEAD

This morning I saw my father driving a red
Toyota wagon with Quebec plates, *je me
souviens,* turning the corner at Grand, heading

west. He didn't see me, and I was surprised
to see him in the city without calling on me
even though, for the last three years, he has been

dead. It certainly looked like him, the chiselled
jaw, the Grecian formula hair, yes, my father
maybe twenty years ago, still in his prime, still

himself, or looking like himself. All
the immortality the Earth can offer
may be the kind we had before

we were even born, the living we did then,
we will continue to do through genes
we also share with Neanderthals.

My father drives on not knowing me.
The dead are not dead, perhaps
the dead are not even transformed. They are

everywhere, just not talking to us.
Don't try listening for them in family photos,
if they are forever, they are forever

dumb with forgotten conversations when
every day is that August day in 1992. My father
in his white-striped polo shirt,

high in the boughs of a fig tree, gathering fruit
for my greed. I still see him in many places,
and in my hands, my Roman nose, and chiselled jaw.

As a pear repeats itself, each time a little altered,
On every branch of a tree.[1] Our dead
have retired and moved off island.

They are not gone, they have not passed on,
they are incommunicado.

---

1 *Lines from Jane Hirschfield's poem, "Great Powers Once Raged Through Your Body"*

THE POSSIBILITY OF TIME TRAVEL

Summer afternoon. Summer
afternoon, the woman, not yet
old, lies on her bed naked

under a ceiling fan.
Such humidity and heat.
The air steams with no

visible vapour. She is resting,
but restless. A ringing
from the street, a bell, close

and then closer. Incessant
ringing, the knife sharpener
is at her door. The fan keeps on

turning overhead, the blades
blurring. She sees where they are,
where they were, she sees where

they will be. Maybe time is not
an arrow after all but a whirling
storm about to touch down, dire

yet humdrum, a rotating fan,
a grinding stone, a wheel
where Tony sharpens our knives.

LA VITA VECCHIA

The night's smell of horses
     is another way.
Let me tell you again what I think.
The night writes the vita of duckweed
and lodges it in the blue codex below the ground.
    — TIM LILBURN, "THIS"

She has stopped at this spot before on the land
that owns her. Car left by the side of the road, engine running,
she moves in the glow of headlights, orange yellow
like that gibbous moon overhead. She stumbles on the gravel.
That gargling sound is a creek, some ragged shadows, bushes,
rustle with wind, while, perfectly oblong, the baled hay
lies wrapped in silence in the open field. Starlit, moonlit,
in another dimension called time she is a girl in the house
she dreamed of leaving for the emerald city, now she prays
the night's smell of horses
        is another way

to trade in new dreams for old. To return. To take back her name.
When she drove through town she saw only strangers.
She knew no one, no one knew her, though once upon a time
she was born in the county. Was bused to school
with the Browns, the Joneses, the Mitchells, and in her final year,
crowned queen of the prom, and proclaimed, oh so *pretty in pink,*
they all said it, her girlfriends, her boyfriend. Where
are they to be found today? Still haunting the bar on the outskirts
of town where the underage could always sneak a drink?
Let me tell you again what I think

about her coming back or trying to: *it's too little, too late,*
she should give up on it, that's what everybody says, but now
that her father's dead and the farm is sold, she wants something
that's gone. She heads back towards the car, making
her way through a pasture, with nettles and thistles thrashing
her legs, every step a flagellation, exacting penitence.
She is the seed fallen on rocky ground. She is the prodigal
who stayed away and will have no share in the harvest.
That's the truth, find it in the good book, all you'll ever need.
The night writes the vita of duckweed.

La Vita Nuova is just some poor guy's story
about first love, best love, that she read in college. But this
flat land, these sad plots, with their rough-hewn tablets,
the commandments of the father scorched on,
these once fertile fields, all she knew, all she'll truly know
of herself is grit blowing into her eyes, the topsoil, unbound.
But — she is still her father's daughter. She belongs here
and like Jesus in some movie she pulls a thumping, thorn-
      crowned
heart out of her chest, without making a sound,
and lodges it in the blue codex below the ground.

THE TASTE OF LOSS

With the first sip of dark espresso
in the morning I think of her —
how we would drink it together

and she said I always took too long
      and let it go cold.
Another winter of her absence

and spring to come again without her.
A white squirrel chatters on the back porch,
a pumpkin, half-gnawed, frozen there.

Azure sky above, sunlight on the snow.
From the bare lilac, a cardinal whistles,
      a chickadee dee dees.

I stay in all this New-Year's-Eve-day,
loss, the mineral salt taste in my mouth.
Turn it into a glass of ice water

I can down in one drink. I take it
in my hand, bring it to my lips, the smooth glass,
I know that burning cold, I know it.

. . . AND THEN SHE WOKE UP

The last time she saw her parents alive
was in a dream. When she arrived at the house,
it was not the condo in Italy,

nor the nursing home where they died,
but the bungalow in North York, turned
into a rickety shack and balanced on

the edge of a precipice, and the only
way to enter was to cross an abyss
by way of a frayed bamboo bridge, gaping

with holes. Her parents smiled sadly at her
from the other side, shaking their heads
as if to say no, not this time, not yet,

and though she longed to embrace them
for that one last time that is always denied
to the living left behind, she dithered

too fearful to even look down . . .

TURNING THIRTY TWICE OVER

Mishima swore he'd die young,
he wanted to leave a beautiful

corpse. Still alive at forty-five
he committed seppuku.

It was the age, the sixties
feared the thirties.

At thirtysomething you got over it,
and now that you approach thirty

twice over, not a corpse yet
no longer beautiful,

you have stopped
reading Mishima.

BLACK DOG

I had yet to use the selfie stick I got for Christmas
so I took this photo when I could not find the words
for even my empty coffee cup Chez Fred. The tattooed

barista, all piercings, and black torn stockings, fills it up;
always *americano lungo, s'il vous plaît.* What makes
a Parisian lawyer open a bakery in *Montréal?*

The run off in gutters is icing over again and
that's what they call *le printemps* in this city, *n'est-ce pas?*
After twenty-five years of planning, the Egyptian themed

theatre up the street has yet to reopen. Anubis
presides over its grave, not its rebirth. Anubis is
a god with the head of a black dog. Beware of the god.

I sort through stacks of newspapers left behind, the read and
the unread. I like that it's quiet, and the aromas
of espresso and madeleine, the loudest things. I open

the door to a medley of crows calling, no, it's seagulls,
and a dog, tied outside BBP Orthopedics, barking.
Nobody likes to be left alone. It's St. Patrick's Day, or

it was not too long ago, shamrock stickers still plaster
the windows of Liquid Lounge. There's a family picture
taken in Belgium, my brother swaddled in a carriage;

when my mother started to lose her memory she kept
this photo in her pocket; it's folded into quarters
and badly creased. Some might say it was ruined. Red mail truck, red

mailbox, it's a cheerful colour on a dull day in No
Damned Good. How did I get here? I grow old, I grow old, I
will wear the bottoms of my blue jeans rolled. Clouds are pinking

in a cerulean sky; I wax poetic. I am not
home yet where another era's technologies: the Sony
cassette player, the Olivetti typewriter, and my

sixty-five-year-old brain *ne marchent pas bien*. What of the bowl
on the desk, filled with pine cones? No trees will grow from them.
I've set up a little shrine around the folded family

photo I flattened out and then framed. After death there is
an aura, a palpable halo around the faces
in photos of the departed; their silence says *this once was*.

ii

LIFE SENTENCES

*Il poeta e come un minatore scava dentro di se finche
trova un fondo comune a tuti gli uomini.*
— GIORGIO CAPRONI

*The poet is like a miner digging within himself
until he finds depths shared with all mankind.*

LIFE SENTENCES
(An Autobiography in Verse)

1

The past is that far
country you emigrated from
as a child.

2

A-bomb day —
not even Stevenson would've traded
his birthday for yours.

3

Mamma says don't touch
the iron; you're quick to learn
the meaning of hot.

4

Surprised by the burning
bite in the beauty of a rose-
red radish.

5

Mamma hits you
with — what was it — a frying pan
for writing with your left hand?

6

You're Shirley Temple
dancing in the piazza, but nobody
locks you in the closet.

7

If gypsies snatch children,
why does your mother dress you up
as one for *Carnevale*?

8

"Pull down your panties,"
trapped in the stairwell, you do it
so he'll go away.

9

Evenings gallivanting
with Pappa, you learn to pee
squatting at urinals.

10

At the shooting range
Pappa wins you a kewpie doll
dressed in pink feathers.

11

Gone a year in America,
who is this man, and where is
your real father?

12

If hell is hot
then heaven's not, you might as well
move to Canada.

13

Maria Luisa's
too hard to say so teacher renames you
Mary.

14

Life sentence:
you buy *The Prisoner of Zenda* at Coles
for ten cents.

15

Shameful
how you let him touch you there
until you pee.

16

The thing you do
for a stick of Doublemint gum,
the thing!

17

Double your pleasure
double your fun, Double-
mint gum!

18

Sixty-four shades
of Crayola, staying within the lines
feels safe.

19

God's stuck on the roof
of your mouth, you daren't peel back
the wafer with your tongue.

20

Catechism was taught first thing on the curriculum at
St. Thomas Aquinas elementary school . . .

Your inmost thoughts will
all be exposed on Judgment Day —
you're afraid to think!

21

Reading the Narnia
story, you want to eat it too —
Turkish delight.

22

It's a mystery,
when you dig up the mouse,
there's no body, no bones.

23

Not true,
your brother says you were just
too afraid to look.

24

Twenty-three cents saved,
you and your brother run
away from home.

25

Twenty-three cents buys
two chocolate bars, three gum balls,
hungry, you go home.

26

Your mother starved in a concentration camp during
the Second World War . . .

For spending your savings
on comics, Mother hits you
with a bread loaf.

27

Atomic warning system drills:
everybody ducks and hides
under the desks.

28

They announce it
over the PA: *President Kennedy's*
been shot.

29

Who are you really
when your birth certificate's
written in pencil?

30

Writing
nose so close to the page, teacher says
you'll need glasses.

31

In grade five you know
the boy who hits you with your *Oxford Concise*
loves you.

32

At ten you have breasts
Philip pokes with the pointer
to see if they're real.

33

You pronounce your name
Dee-mee-shell as if it were,
though it's not, French.

34

You visit relatives
in Cleveland who have changed
their name to Mitchell.

35

(Not) surprisingly
your first job's a page
in the library!

36

Your first paycheque
buys that blue silk blouse
with pearl buttons.

37

In high school
you stay home sick a lot and hit
the *marsala*.

38

Among the offspring
of Jewish doctors you're known
as Miraculous Mary.

39

Shame in Dostoevsky
Dimitri's feet, Brother Andre's corpse
starting to stink.

40

"Get your nose
out of that book and wash the dishes,
dust the furniture!"

41

"Why go to university
when you can teach grade school
or get married?"

42

According to Pierre Bayard's theory:
to every book you read you bring your idea of the book,
to every story you read you bring your story . . .

War and Peace is
that food fight in the kitchen —
ketchup on the wall.

43

Working at A&W
you don't see the moon landing
broadcast in real time.

44

In the age of Twiggy
you're size eighteen but hip
dressed in a muumuu.

45

You much prefer
food to sex, it doesn't
bite back.

46

La Belle Dame sans Merci —
you learn to speak the language
of the dark muse.

47

Everywhere
and nowhere, the white
whale.

48

In the crystal ball
you're shown great fame while in life
grateful obscurity.

49

All the professors
have British accents, so cool,
so post-colonial.

50

Ruth and Carlo,
you only ever have
two friends.

51

You read loudly
scenes from *Women in Love*, not knowing
they're about sex.

52

He's as pretty
as Paul McCartney; *love, love me do* . . .
he does not.

53

The A+ student
skips lectures to read standing up
in the library stacks.

54

No actor,
you're stuck on props for *Six Characters
in Search of an Author*.

55

There's no satisfying
hunger for that grilled cheese sandwich
with Christ's face.

56

Miss Lanciano —
you read a poem as your talent
and come in fourth.

57

Like Bartleby
the Scrivener, you would prefer
not to . . .

58

Offering you a ride
the guy in the Porsche yells he's doing you
a favour.

59

Your life's soundtrack:
short people got, short people
got no reason to live . . .

60

Not deserving love
you marry the man who doesn't
love you.

61

It's a girl —
giving birth you feel truly female
for the first time.

62

You're an editor
at *Toronto Life* accepting poems
by the inch.

63

Divorce —
the chef's knife is his and wants
sharpening.

64

One by one
your husband's friends come to give you
what he would not.

65

Poems about birth
shut men out, you're told
death's universal.

66

Your daughter falls out of the stroller and bashes her nose . . .

you were a baby
when Mamma tripped, she didn't
push you down the stairs.

67

The eighties —
David Byrne in his big white suit;
you in your skin.

68

Obasan absolves you;
it's not yours, it's Old Man Gower's fault,
Naomi!

69

You tack up bedsheets
for drapes still Mother no longer calls you
a gypsy.

70

Tenure —
is it that golden gate shutting
against your writing?

71

The poems that come
most easily to you are written
by someone else.

72

Leo like Napoleon
you're shorter than your stature and suffer
stomach pain.

73

You and your daughter jump out the train window.
 After the Brighton disaster Via Rail implements
  procedures in case of fire on its passenger lines . . .

Reading Neruda's
"La Muerte" on a burning train,
living to reread it.

74

Poems and semicolons
always on the next page;
vast vistas . . .

75

Bonjour, *good day,*
comment ça va;
how goes it?

76

Don't write
what you can shout; write what
shuts you up.

(after Yannis Ritsos)

77

Your sister; your daughter;
then one Christmas your father
overdoses on Tylenol.

78

Every weekend
he dances with his wife, the man
you declined to marry.

79

An antique bust
serves both as bookend
and your hat stand.

80

Moonlight also
glows on the tarnished silverware —
that's why you write.

81

Mamma says: *"Salute
la tua figlia"*; Pappa says: "I would
but I'm not here."

82

Capable
the word you use in your mother's eulogy feels
no small praise.

83

Your mother's blouse
in the memory box, does it still
smell faintly of her?

84

Out of Alzheimer's
comes your father's warning:
"Don't you be a soldier!"

85

Emptied
of meaning words fill up
with themselves.

     (after Yannis Ritsos)

86

I like to hear the sound
of form, and I like to hear
the sound of it breaking.
(Frederick Seidel)

87

Your madeleines are
Chiquita bananas Pappa would bring
home from work.

88

Mi manca l'italia
but when you return it's as if you'd never been
born in that country.

89

Faulkner wrote: The past is never dead. It's not even past.

Even the sunlight
warming your face now is
from eight minutes ago.

90

Mary, you can't go
back to yesterday, you were
a different person then.

91
Old friend
when did you start speaking of yourself
in the third person?

92
At sixty-six
you're still doing the moonwalk
to warm up.

93
Aging —
walking the dog past a mirror
you recognize the dog!

94
Words —
all the windows in the house are
frosted.

95
Swatting the half moon
on the calendar, what good are
those new glasses!

96

Dear Pappa,
I (always) remember your birthday,
not your death day.

97

This living hand, now warm and capable
again and again, longing to take yours,
John Keats.

98

Twenty-five autumns
in Montreal, still the question,
where's home?

99

Oqurum,
the only surviving word of Khazar,
meaning: "I have read."

100

One hundred sentences
just to say you've been on Earth —
however briefly!

iii

AFTER

Lit up blue by the strangeness of god.

— ALICE OSWALD

LIKE KAFKA'S APE
(After Giorgio Caproni)

*. . . your life as apes, gentlemen, in so far as something of that kind lies
behind you, cannot be farther removed from you than mine is from me.*

No, it's not mine
this country I was shipped to,
not born in. Now
even among the crowds
I'm at a loss and lonesome,
I'm an outlier, an anomaly like
a stained-glass angel in the church
of There's No God. Like
a human on exhibit in the zoo.

In my heart there's another country
I long for. It's somewhere *al di là*
in the idea of a memory, a hometown,
a city, gloomy by day, but by night
all aglimmer with lights, trembling like
yahrzeit candles lit for the living.
When the moon rises, resplendent
over the cemetery, the young go
there to boogie among the tombs. O city,

O country, where none, not death, not
the devil can ever take me back.

THE LIGHT IN EACH OF US
(After Giorgio Caproni)

My grandmother lived in a neighbouring village
high in the Apennine mountains, I remember we took the bus
to visit her and the diesel smell made me ill.

I remember the church behind my grandmother's house,
after the bombs fell, the bell tower was rebuilt to the side.
You could see the sound of the bells ringing.

That year my father was in Canada and lonely
for him, we visited my grandmother a lot.
I remember waiting for the bus to return home.

My mother's dark hair was shot red with sunlight,
her brown eyes turned green. The sky was below us,

                                                    not above,

and the birds, swooping for crumbs, were myriad.
I was a very small child then and tired
so we sat waiting on some stone steps

nodding, my mother and I, as if
we had no place to sleep.
When the bus finally came we

roused ourselves, astonished to see
the light in each bird
snuffed out by the stars.

EVENING LIGHT
(After Umberto Saba)

Moon rise.
               In the street it's still
day though dusk's rapidly descending.
The young don't notice, they're busy
texting, faces lit up
by the screens. They have no idea
about death, how in the end, it's

                                  what helps you live.

THE BLUE BOWING OF EVENING
(After Dino Campana)

I sing the blue bowing of evening

The bowing of darkening evenings

That Kamouraska sang

In a broken down little pastoral song

Among the maples on the dark embankment of evening

That Kamouraska sang

Among the maples on the dark embankment of evening

Broken down little Québécois pastoral song

That Kamouraska sang

ARS POETICA
(After Dino Campana)

Writing, writing, and writhing —
I prefer not to, I prefer to
listen, yes, listen to the ocean
shushing the shore and more. Poetry's
writing and erasing, writing and erasing
is all one solitary operation —
and that's all I know about nothing.

ON STYLE
(After Dino Campana)

My verses are marvellous for somebody
Though they may chink like dollar store trash
It's a grand illusion; they are created
From stuff you're sure to like
A dutiful daughter is not bound
To sew new dresses every day
She has one style, she shows off her figure
And tries her best not to look dowdy
You don't know how to get by without
Haute couture? You would like it dished out
Like *cuisine minceur,* on a fancy plate?
If you gave it some thought you would be
Embarrassed by your accessories, for our
Human dignity. F. T. Marinetti (like George Dubya)
At a certain juncture said: the Futurist designer
Designs jeans for the war, the designer
Who specializes in such specialties
I'll keep on wearing them and if they get torn
They will still be trendy for being so
And where there are tears in the cloth
Smog and the love of freedom
Will cover me up, and so I have worn
Plenty of thrift-shop cast-offs
Dressed in what's cheap and comfortable
Hanging out in too cool rags, practically in the buff
But if my threads are dreadful
The heart of this poet is nonetheless natty
On its own, and you might have known that

If you were a believer or had a modicum
Of humanity
My verses are marvellous for somebody
Though they may chink like dollar store trash
It's a grand illusion; they are created
from stuff you're sure to like

BED OF ROSES
(After Dino Campana)

In a moment the roses
Faded
Petals dropped from the roses

Because I could not forget the roses
We looked for them together
And so we found some roses

They were your roses they were my roses
This garden we called love
From our blood and tears sprang roses

Among the briars we plucked roses
Glistening for a moment in the morning sun
Roses that were not our roses

My roses your roses —
The I-forget-whose roses

LIFE IS A ROSE
(Ronsard V)

When you are old and sitting by the fire
sleepily reading some book of poetry
until you come across this poem and cry:
"How that poet raved about my beauty!"

Your house will be empty then, your children
grown, your husband senile, but as my moniker
parts your lips you will smile, oh to have been
so loved, to have been immortalized by desire.

I will be dead, just a few bones crumbling
under the myrtle, while you will be still warm,
cozy in your chair, but wistful and wishing
you hadn't rejected me that summer,

so love me now, before your loveliness
withers, life is a rose — then nothingness.

ON THE WAY TO THE VILLAGE STEAM BATHS
(After Pier Paolo Pasolini)

They're heading for the steam baths in the Village,
guys on bicycles,
mountain bikes or Bixis, with their boyish
goodness and their boyish badness
hiding, or flaunting, they're indifferent
to what's in the warmth at the crotch of their jeans,
secret . . . hard-ons.
Long haired or buzz cut, sporting bright T-shirts,
they flare in the night, in a merry-go-
roundabout, they razzle-dazzle the dark
these fabulous knights of the night . . .

They're heading for the steam baths in the Village.
That one's riding high, as if at home
on the steppes of Russia, on the goat trails in Mexico,
on the hog farms of Saint-Cuthbert, of Saint-Martin
in the muck smelling of shit and Lenten ashes,
toque pulled down to the eyeline.
He left the farm at sixteen
and now he's a joker
with a sin city smile, though he still tastes
of pork and beans and maple syrup . . .

That one too is heading for the Village steam baths
he's a breadwinner who's been laid off
at Bombardier, his body creaks,
the joints rub bone on bone, his body's
a scrap metal heap moving as if remotely

controlled. He's dressed in torn jeans
but not the designer kind. He lights up a fag
end, that's all that's left of his beginnings,
sputtering now like an ember in an urn.
He can't die if he's never been born.

They won't die if they've never been born
on the way to the Village steam baths . . .

THE BIG BANG

(while someone from afar off
blows birthday candles for the world.
     – IRVING LAYTON)

In the beginning was a sparkler with no heat.
The big bang was silent, and in the silence,
a great cake with a billion candles was carried
weightlessly into a dark room.

Your grandmother, a bit confused about where
she is and who you all are, is wheezing, waiting
for she knows not what, for someone from above
to blow out birthday candles for the world.

ENIGMATICO REVISITED

One summer, oh eons ago, you came back
for the first time to that olive and sun-drenched
land of your birth. Why was it so romantic

then to dance at midnight among graves?
That gang of you, *ragazzi e ragazze,*
chaperoned by an aunt, half a child herself.

His skin, bronzed, his hair, streaked with gold,
Adonis picked a white flower, tucked it
behind your ear, where it glowed, ghostly,

moonlight licking at it. That *contadino,*
half god, asked you to marry him, but you
were a tourist to village life. Blame Camus,

blame de Beauvoir, blame your reading,
it made you a stranger to what was wanted
then of women. To what you wanted really.

Now, on your umpteenth return, nothing
seems changed except yourself. He stopped
asking after you years before. Now you ask

after him. You did not aspire to that life
where every weekend he dances with his wife,
they dance best who dance with desire.

DE SICA'S *LADRI DI BICICLETTE*

I can no longer get past that scene
where Maria pawns her matrimonial linen,
a poor woman's dowry, and so precious
to her, while in the background there are
piles of such bedsheets at the shop.
They have no money and her husband
Antonio needs a bicycle to get a job
putting up posters around the city.
It pays good money every week, they can
even buy an egg for their first-born
daughter — no, that's not in the movie,
that was my family in postwar Italy. I remember

the first egg. My mother punctured the top
with a needle and I drank it down raw.

ROBERT LOWELL READS AT SCARBOROUGH COLLEGE, CIRCA 1970

An audience of one came to hear the renowned
poet read, if you do not count the coterie of three
accompanying him, so they left the lecture room
for an open lounge in the hall. The building
— a titanic monolith — was itself of interest
and worth the move to view walls rising in slabs
of concrete. Even the windows were bulwarks
of glass through which light leaked, snow filtered light
falling from the firmament and about to flatten

the world. They sat, the three, along with one student
come to see a real poet, a living one, with a sense
that she was about to partake of a sacrament,
a mystery. To prepare herself she had read him,
standing in the library stacks. The poet
was about to manifest. The word, so fragile, so

friable, made flesh. He stood — nor did he seem aggrieved
to speak to so few — his book holding him up.
A bit of preamble on the Cuban Missile
Crisis and what it means, what it meant, to live
in the shadow of nuclear annihilation,
a sky about to fall on us all, and end
life as we know it. He was right to be depressed,
it was far more than brain chemistry at work.
His poetry was not political, but he had been
a fire-breathing Catholic C.O. — or so he confessed

in "Memories of West Street and Lepke." Head angled
in Modigliani melancholy or as if a violin
were propped between shoulder and chin,
Lowell read as if he were listening
to someone else, some invisible other reading.

More than forty years later now does she still
imagine him, eyes fixed on the printed lines of his page,
and literally seeing *the blue threads as thin as pen-writing*
on his father's bedspread? Did he scry there his last
moments: New York City, in a taxi, on the way back
to Elizabeth, the critic spouse? There were three wives,
one always lovelier than the last, three times
the whoop, the wail, the woe that is in marriage. Until

he looked back and saw what he could not see then,
what cannot be seen head-on with looking.

A POEM ABOUT ABSOLUTELY NOTHING

"I have done absolutely nothing
for six weeks," in a letter to Woolf,
Eliot admonishes himself, "I have been
boiled in a hell broth." He was referring
to his mother's visit. All day I too
have done nothing.

                      Who begins a letter
that way? or, for that matter, a poem?
The aspen admonishes, the spruce censures
me. I have been advised, sagely, as a woman
to wear pink, it will disarm my enemies.

DEATH AND TRANSFIGURATION IN NEW YORK CITY
(An Essay in Verse)

JUNE 11, 2001

i Mulberry Time
*(Homesick, I jog in Central Park, larger
than Mont Royal, also Olmsted designed)*

Here at the centre of the concrete city find
refuge for green, for lakes and for loons.
I think they're loons the way they dive

then disappear below the glimmering surface
of the water. I watch for them as I run forlorn
around the reservoir named Jackie Onassis.

*There'll be great presidents
again, but there'll never be another Camelot.*
There'll never be another Guenivere,

our first lady in her Chanel suits. We miss
her. What we name to commemorate,
what we name to remember is the absence

of greatness. On the path, on the beaten earth
path, I run in mulberry time. I make jam
underfoot. There's more fruit, more fruit

than even the birds can devour.
As ravenous as pterodactyls
in the sky above us airplanes wheel.

White plumes trail from their tails,
long plumes of white smoke
rising over the skyline of New York.

ii The Last Word Is Silence

(I listen to the radio, as my heart pumps, another stops)

It's 7:14 a.m. and already hot,
on an overcast morning in June
74 degrees Fahrenheit and rising.
President Bush presides over
the first federal execution since 1963.
This is something he's good at,
he's had a lot of practice. As governor
of Texas he sent 140 to their deaths.

What we name to commemorate,
what we mean when we remember the dead —

This morning we're pushing someone along
to the other side who himself pushed 168.
Numbers, numbers. There are faces behind
these numbers. Faces from America's Kids
the daycare where McVeigh parked his truck
bomb.²
So you see it's fair,
so you see it's just
and now it's his turn to die.

McVeigh is silent. There are no last
words. On death row.

The unrepentant, let us not call him a man,

---

2 *In some reports, McVeigh is described as lamenting the collateral damage
caused by this choice.*

let us call him evildoer, criminal, terrorist,
jailbird, murderer — let us call him insane,
he who calls himself a libertarian. Let us not name
him by the name you might give to your own son,
Timmy. To watch a son die —

to wait for it. They were not
waiting for the bomb, the children in Oklahoma City,
they were waiting in the nursery for the teacher
to distribute the crayons.

Nineteen children were killed in the bombing.
Nineteen not alive now to vote against
the execution the liberals lament, the liberals
who don't understand war has been declared
in their own country.
An eye for an eye is retribution,
but when so many are dead, and the man only
has two? Two across the screens of a nation
multiplied might satisfy.

The evildoer is all-American.
Blond. Clean-cut. Cooperative
with the guards as he is strapped onto a gurney.
He makes eye contact with each of the witnesses.
He is silent. A flicker of his fingers.
An easing of his legs in the chair.

A man, unrepentant, the reporter reports.
McVeigh glares at the camera.
He turns away from the injected death,
turns away from the 24-inch screen
as justice is telecast for those who watch
650 miles away for justice to be done.

He looks up at the ceiling. He dies
with his eyes open.

iii *Tod und Verklärung*
(some believe that only music can truly speak for us)

June 11 and WQXR commemorates
Richard Strauss's birthday by playing *Death
and Transfiguration.* When he wrote the symphonic
poem, Strauss was in good health,
young and far from his own end in another
century. An old burgher lying on a bed lit
by candles was a remote fantasy. In his youth
an old man dreaming of his youth. Strauss was
not then Reichsmusikkammer in Hitler's Germany
using his music to save the Jewish grandchildren,
music that failed to save so many others.

A crescendo,
then a diminuendo.

The burgher is lucky to die in his own room
with no eyes watching him from the walls.
He remembers love, not war and desert storms,
he remembers green fields, not blood
though he picks red poppy, yellow broom
for a bouquet he presents to his fiancée.

As the music grows fervent he holds
a woman in his arms — not a rifle.
He recalls embraces, not explosions
from a distance. But when the music fades
again love is gone. He's back on the sickbed.

He's strapped on a gurney.
Then in the chair. With the lethal injection
his pulse slows, his vision blurs,
and he slips into silence, along with the music
into near silence — that tells us

with death there is release from the world
and then transfiguration.

in   Of Chickens and Men
(some ignore the death of the guy linked to white supremacists)

A slight turn of the radio dial is a move
                                    from the funereal into the farcical.
On KISS.FM the story of the day
is about another kind of unspeakable
crime — a guy arrested for having sex
in a hotel room with a chicken.
The blood, the feathers, tipped
off the chambermaid. Now the man's in jail
because you can't have sex in a hotel room
with a chicken. It's illegal.
You can stuff a chicken
with stuffing. You can baste a chicken,
you can marinade a chicken. You can chop,
filet, you can even debone a chicken,
but you can't have sex in a hotel room with a chicken.[3]

From the funereal to the farcical —
Still they care about something human
today they're giving away an iMac computer
to empower some lucky person in their community.

•

It wasn't a statement. McVeigh declined to back
the vegan movement by ordering a vegetarian dish
as his last meal. After all he was a soldier.

---

3 *As remembered from listening to the broadcast.*

He was a huntsman, a trained killer and the fate
of chickens was not part of his mission.
Where do you draw the line? he wrote in response
to Bruce Friedrich of People for the Ethical Treatment of Animals,
Where do those who oppose suffering stand?
Plants are alive too, they react to stimuli (including "pain")
so how about them? To me the answer is
as the Indians believed: respect the life you take
to sustain yourself, come to terms with your place
in the food chain.[4] At the supermarket
how to respect life when it's shrink-wrapped
remains a question. For his last meal
McVeigh ate two pints of chocolate mint
ice cream, but it wasn't meant as a statement.

---

4 *From McVeigh's letter published in* Harper's *before the execution.*

Why I Could Not Write This Poem

(moral clarity as kitsch: leached of history and so of meaning,
we commemorated the six-month anniversary of the death of irony)

You can't have sympathy for a terrorist. On September 11, 2001,
in the light of digital TV we saw the twin towers of World
Trade smoke, burn, then fall. Twin towers, not the twin cities
Hiroshima, Nagasaki. Three short months after the execution and
then this — I imagined that Timothy McVeigh was still waging
war on the federal government. But no, this time the evildoers
were really from the Middle East, although CIA trained, not one
of "US."

I only had notes towards this poem anyway. I had abandoned
poetry for the novel — then poetry abandoned me.

SOMEWHERE I HAVE NEVER TRAVELLED

I arrived at the Canada-US border.
Flags fluttered though there was no wind.
Mine was the sole vehicle at the crossing.

I pulled up to a booth. Nobody
was there. I got out of my car
to peer behind the wicket: darkness

except for the blinking light of a phone.
I had my Canadian passport ready
declaring my Italian birth. The photo

didn't look like me. It felt strange to be
neither here nor there, neither coming
nor going. I arrived at the US-Canada border,

flags the only things moving.
The sun was low but I cast no shadow.

AUTHOR'S NOTES

The poems in this collection dedicated in the "after" mode use translation as a tool for improvisation and conversation. My thefts from poets I admire are in the form of borrowed lines or homage to their work as acknowledged in the notes below.

Many of these poems are autobiographical but they are so in a mode that includes history, culture, and reading as forms of shared experience.

The epigraph to the book as a whole is from John Banville's novel *The Sea*. The first section's epigraph is from James Merrill's last poem, "Christmas Tree," written as he was dying of AIDS; the second section quotes Giorgio Caproni from an interview found online, there are many versions and instances of his use of the metaphor of the poet as miner, finding a shared humanity through digging deep into the self; the third section uses a line from Alice Oswald's book *Memorial*.

"Scotopia" was written in response to Rachel Baird's collaborative art project "Nightfall — An Urban Renga."

"The Mountain After Klein" is a homage to A. M. Klein's poem

"The Mountain" and was written at the invitation of Jason Camlot for *The A. M. Klein Reboot Project.*

The title "The Bicycle Thief" references the 1948 Vittorio De Sica film. The English translation rendered the title, *Ladri di biciclette* or *Bicycle Thieves*, in the singular. In the third part of this collection, the poem "De Sica's *Ladri di biciclette*" is about the film and its significance to me.

In "The Winds of Homecoming," the epigraph is from a poem among Rilke's uncollected poems, "{Ah, not to be cut off}," translated by Stephen Mitchell, *Ahead of All Parting: The Selected Poetry and Prose of Rainer Maria Rilke*, 1995 Modern Library Edition.

"Forgetfulness" owes some of its inspiration and opening moves to a poem by that title from *Late Into the Night*, the last poems of Yannis Ritsos, as translated by Martin McKinsey, Oberlin College 1995. It also owes much to the late Margaret Owen Newson in whose house I stayed for a writer's retreat in the summer of 2013.

"The Montreal Book of the Dead" incorporates two lines from Jane Hirshfield's poem "Great Powers Once Raged Through Your Body," from *Each Happiness Ringed by Lions, Selected Poems*, Bloodaxe, 2005 edition.

"*La Vita Vecchia*" is a glosa on Tim Lilburn's poem "This," from his collection *To the River*, McClelland & Stewart, 1999.

In "Life Sentences" #42, the reference is from an idea about how we read by Pierre Bayard in his book *How to Talk About Books*

You Haven't Read, translated from the French by Jeffrey Mehlman, Raincoast Books, 2007.

#76 and #85 are improvisations on Yannis Ritsos, #78 and #17 from *111 Tristichs/Second Series* and */Third Series* respectively, Pella Publishing, 1990.

The source for #86 is a quotation from the poet in an interview in the *Paris Review*, The Art of Poetry No.95.

In #97, the line is from a John Keats poem found in marginalia, an untitled eight line fragment written by the dying poet.

"Like Kafka's Ape" is an improvisation on Giorgio Caproni's poem "Il gibbone"; the epigraph is from Kafka's story "A Report to an Academy," translated by Willa and Edwin Muir.

"The Light in Each of Us" is an improvisation on Giorgio Caproni's poem "*Ricordo.*"

"Evening Light" is an improvisation on Umberto Saba's poem "*Sera di febbraio.*"

"The Blue Bowing of Evening" is a homage to Dino Campana's lyrical poetry about place in *Canti Orifici.*

"Ars Poetica" is an improvisation on Dino Campana's poem beginning "*fabbricare, fabbricare, fabbricare*" from *Canti Orfici.*

"On Style" is an improvisation on Dino Campana's poem "*I miei versi sono meravigliosi a qualcuno.*"

"Bed of Roses" is a homage to Dino Campana's *Canti Orfici*.

"Life Is a Rose" is a free translation of Ronsard's sonnet *"quand vous serez bien vieille."*

"On the Way to the Village Steam Baths" is a homage or improvisation on Pier Paolo Pasolini's poem *"Verso le terme di Caracalla,"* from *la religione del mio tempo*.

"The Big Bang" uses as epigraph two lines taken from Irving Layton's poem "The Birth of Tragedy."

"Enigmatico Revisited" closes with a line from Irving Layton's poem "Dancing with Desire."

"Robert Lowell Reads at Scarborough College, circa 1970" references two of his poems: "Memories of West Street and Lepke" and "Father's Bedroom."

"A Poem about Absolutely Nothing" uses quotes from a letter written by T. S. Eliot to Virginia Woolf.

The McVeigh letter quoted in "Death and Transfiguration in New York City" can be found in *Harper's*, July 1, 2001.

ACKNOWLEDGEMENTS

Earlier versions of some of these poems have been previously published in *Canadian Poetries*, *CV2*, *Matrix*, *Poetry Quebec*, *The Fiddlehead*, *Truck*, and *Vallum*.

I would like to thank my friends and first readers of these poems, Roo Borson, Kim Maltman, Cameron Hayne, and Susan Gillis. I would also like to thank Bryan Newson for inviting me to stay and write at his mother's house in Comox for a month.

Many thanks too to all at ECW, particularly my editor, Michael Holmes, and the designers for capturing the look of neorealist Italian cinema in the production of this book.

FINE